**HAL LEONARD**  HARMONICA FOR **K**

 AUDIO ACCESS INCLUDED

11 Popular Songs Arranged on Harmonica for Beginners

By Eric Plahna

PLAYBACK+
Speed • Pitch • Balance • Loop

To access audio, visit:
www.halleonard.com/mylibrary
Enter Code
8462-7972-4521-1015

ISBN 978-1-5400-5096-0

For all works contained herein:
Unauthorized copying, arranging, adapting, recording, internet posting, public performance,
or other distribution of the music in this publication is an infringement of copyright.
Infringers are liable under the law.

Visit Hal Leonard Online at **www.halleonard.com**

Explore the entire family of Hal Leonard products and resources

  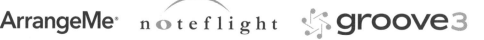 

World headquarters, contact:
Hal Leonard
7777 West Bluemound Road
Milwaukee, WI 53213
Email: info@halleonard.com

In Europe, contact:
Hal Leonard Europe Limited
1 Red Place
London, W1K 6PL
Email: info@halleonardeurope.com

In Australia, contact:
Hal Leonard Australia Pty. Ltd.
4 Lentara Court
Cheltenham, Victoria, 3192 Australia
Email: info@halleonard.com.au

All songs include online audio for download or streaming.
To access the online audio, just head over to **www.halleonard.com/mylibrary**
and input the code found on page 1 of this book!

HOT CROSS BUNS

Traditional

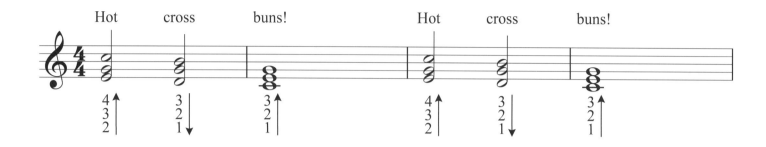

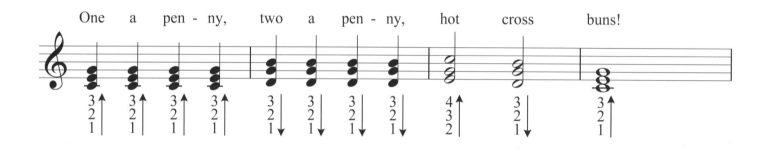

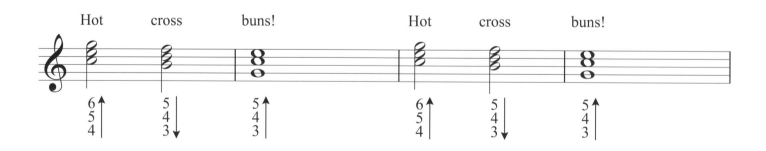

4

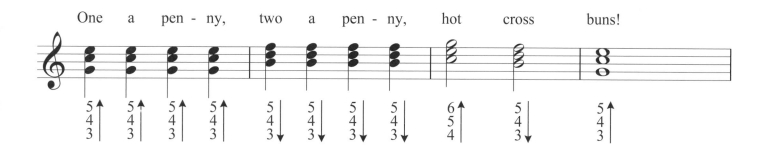

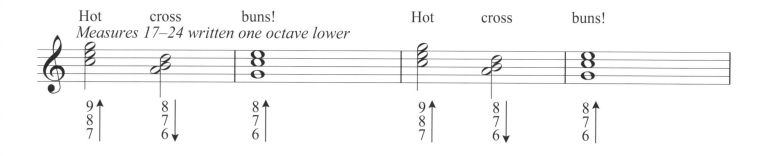

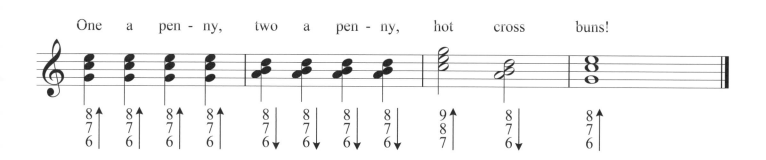

LONG, LONG AGO
(CHORDS)

By THOMAS BAYLY

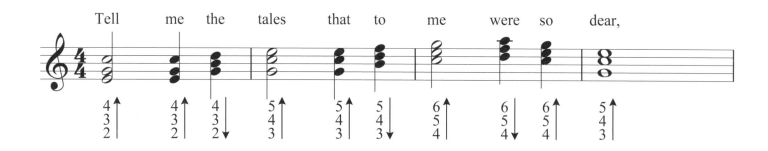

Tell me the tales that to me were so dear,

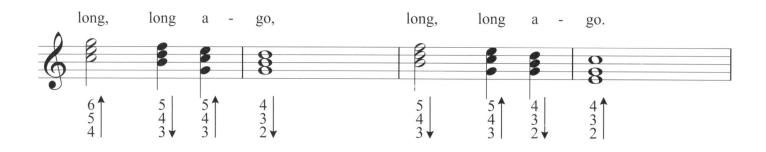

long, long a - go, long, long a - go.

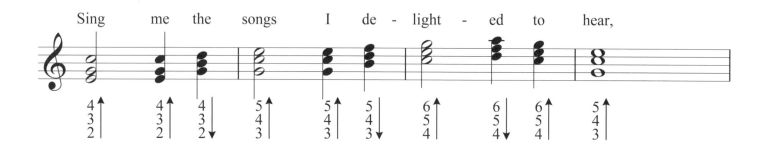

Sing me the songs I de - light - ed to hear,

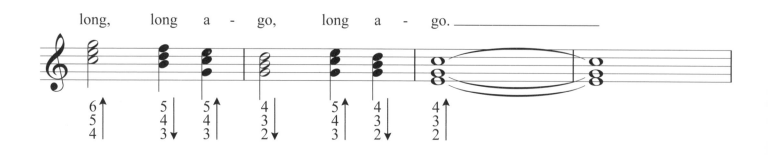

long, long a - go, long a - go. _____

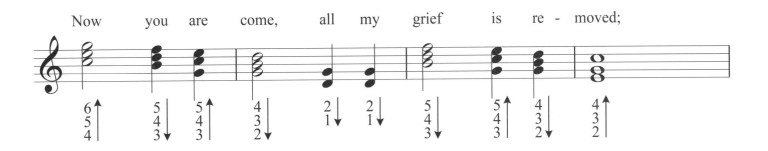

Now you are come, all my grief is re - moved;

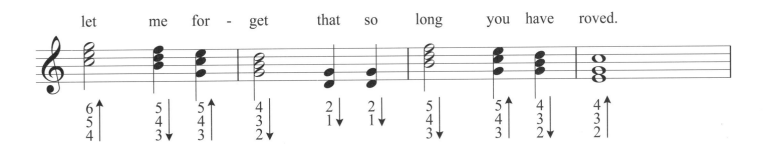

let me for - get that so long you have roved.

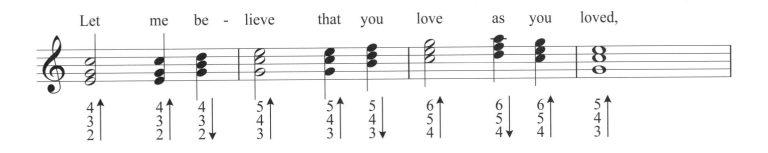

Let me be - lieve that you love as you loved,

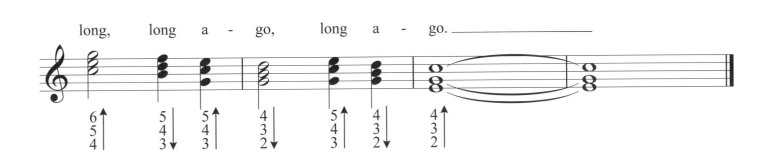

long, long a - go, long a - go.

LONG, LONG AGO
(SINGLE NOTES)

By THOMAS BAYLY

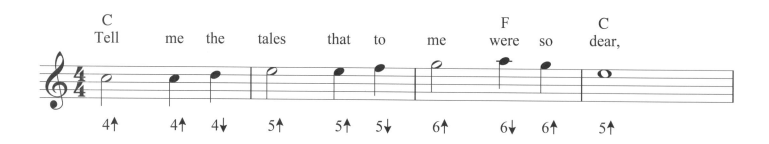

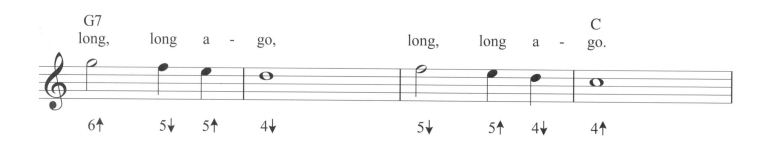

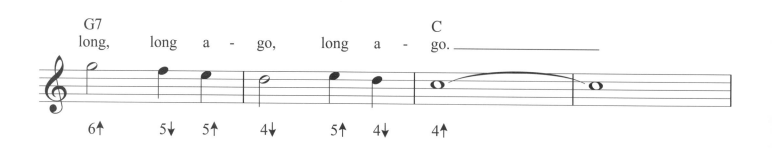

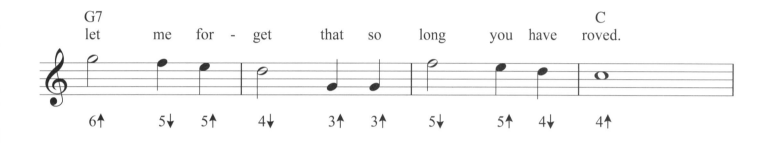

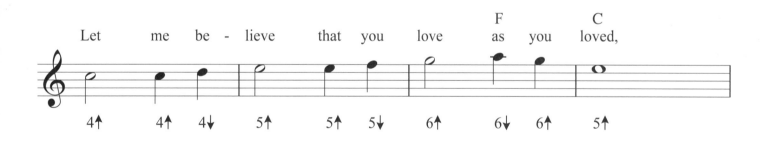

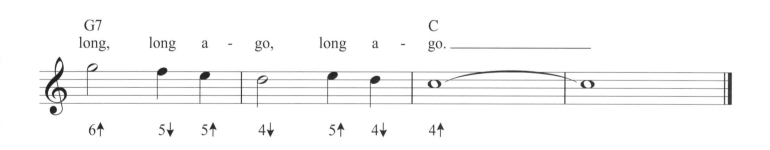

PUFF THE MAGIC DRAGON

Words and Music by LENNY LIPTON
and PETER YARROW

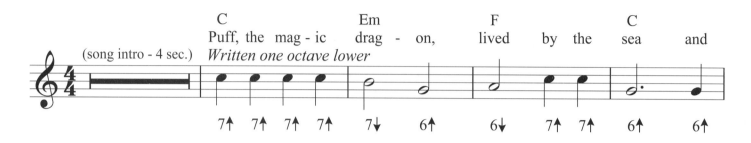

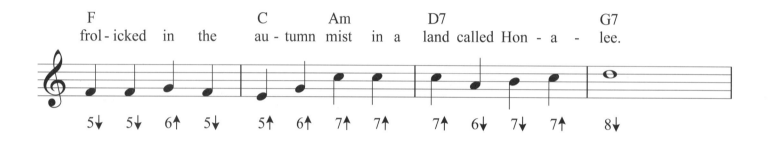

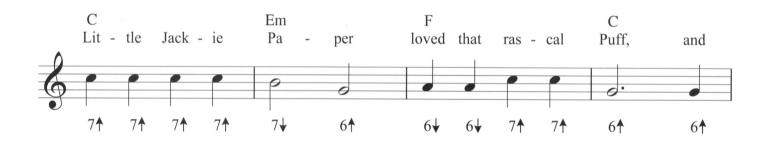

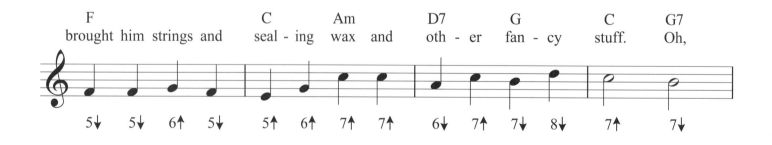

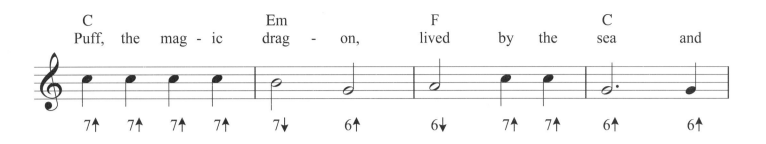

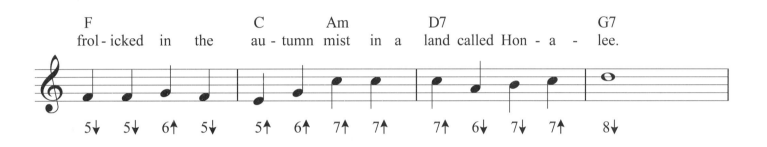

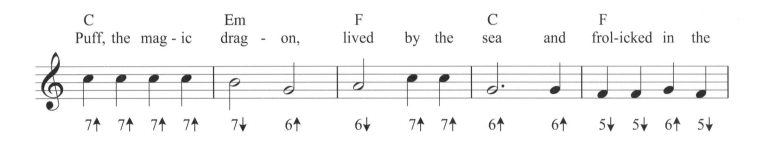

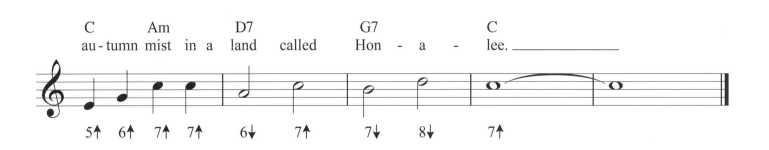

CAN YOU FEEL THE LOVE TONIGHT

from THE LION KING

Music by ELTON JOHN
Lyrics by TIM RICE

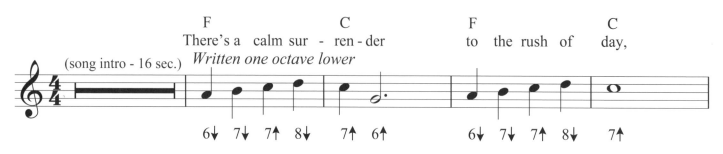

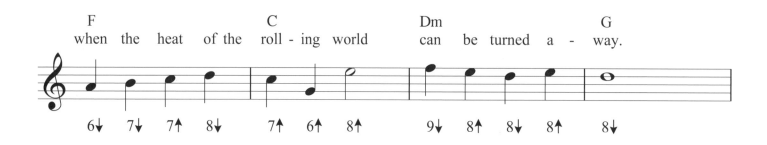

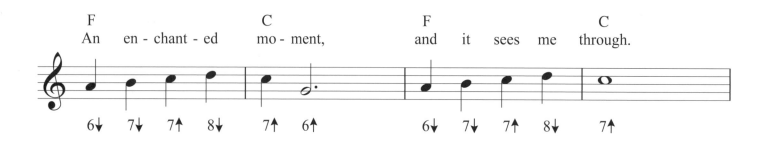

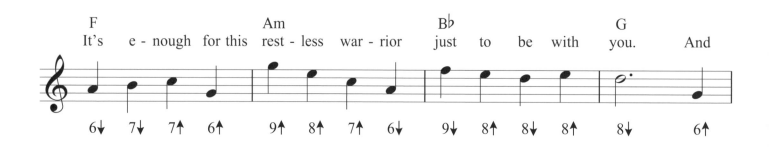

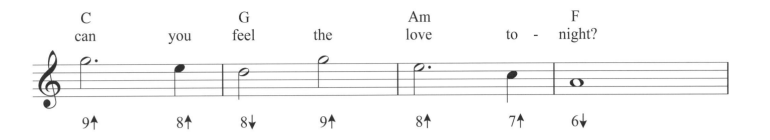

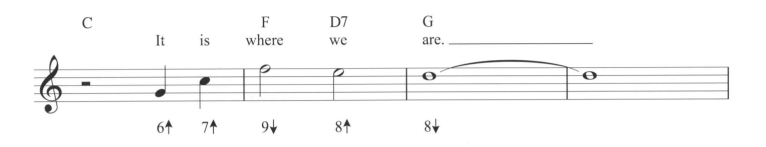

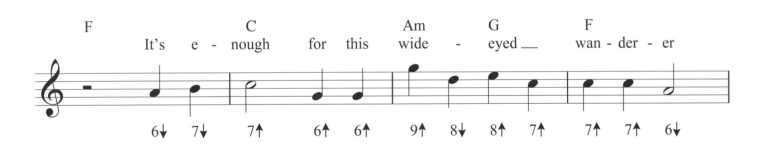

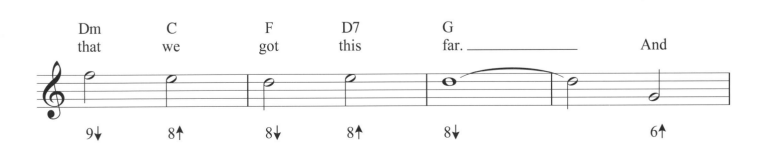

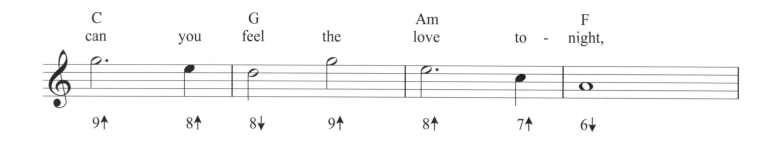

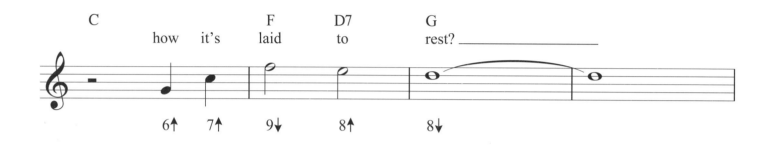

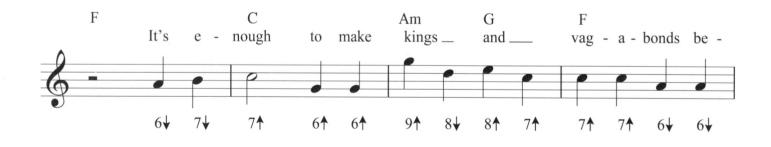

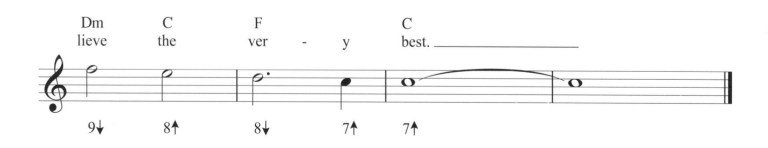

MY HEART WILL GO ON (LOVE THEME FROM 'TITANIC')

from the Paramount and Twentieth Century Fox Motion Picture TITANIC

Music by JAMES HORNER
Lyric by WILL JENNINGS

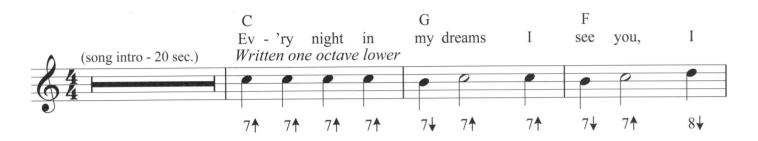

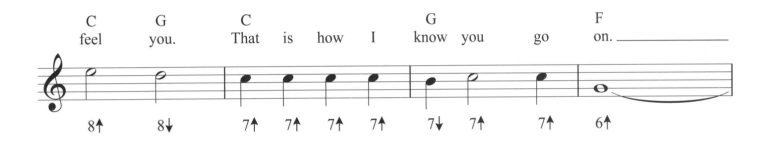

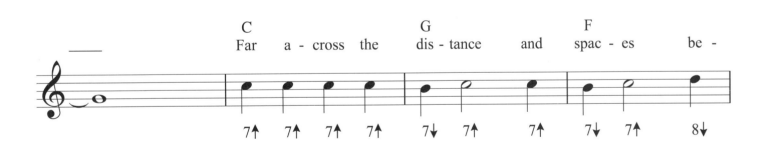

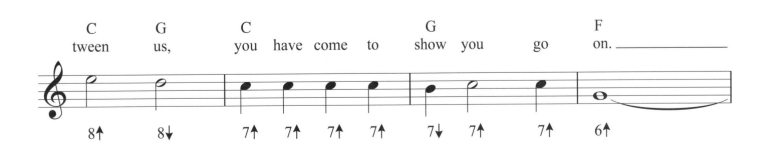

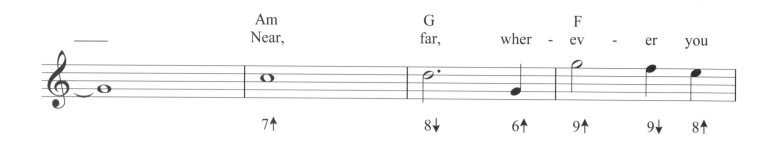

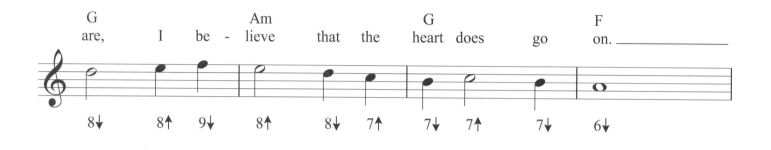

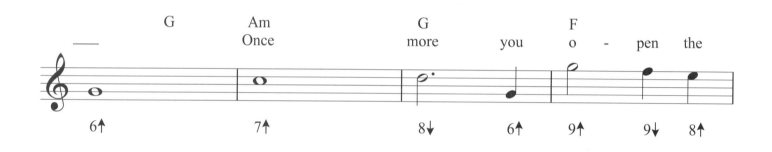

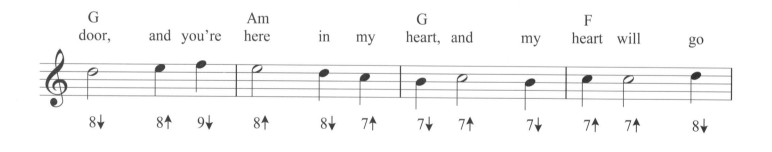

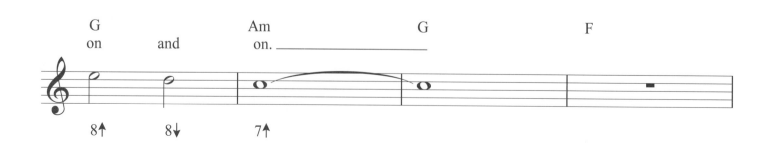

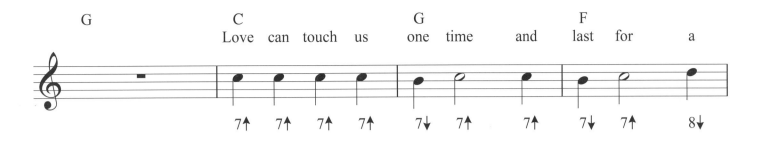

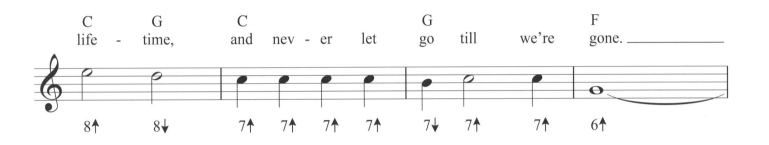

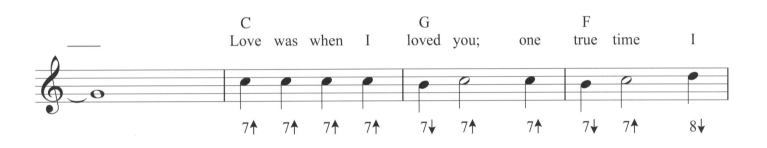

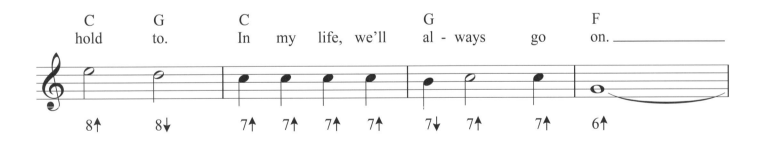

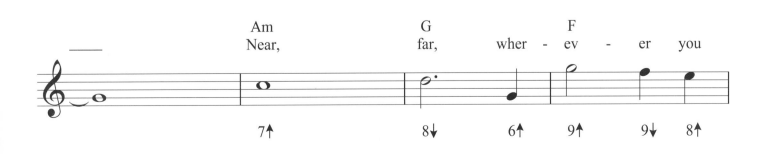

17

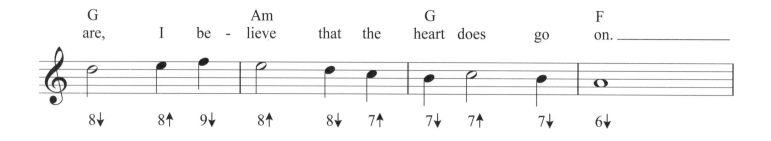

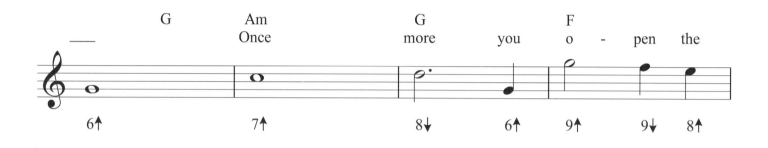

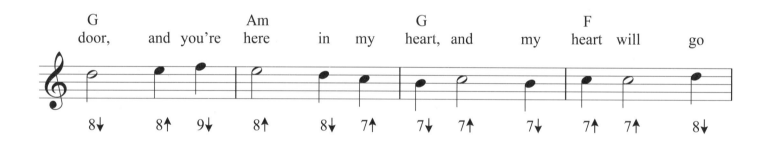

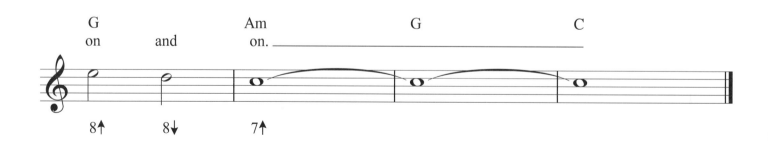

YOUR CHEATIN' HEART

Words and Music by HANK WILLIAMS

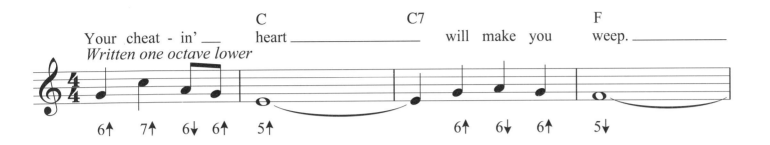

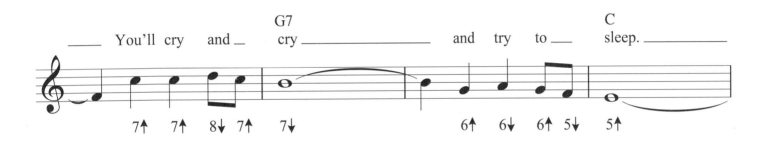

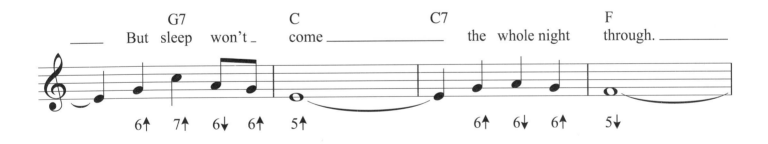

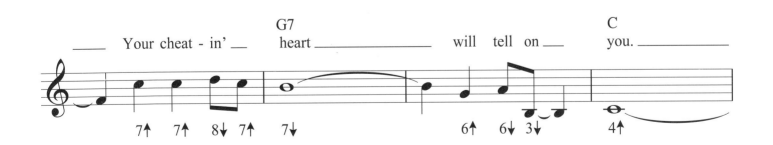

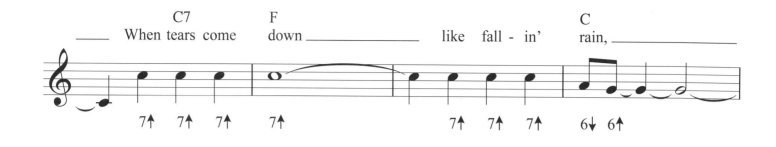

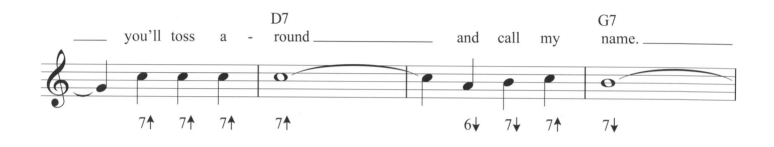

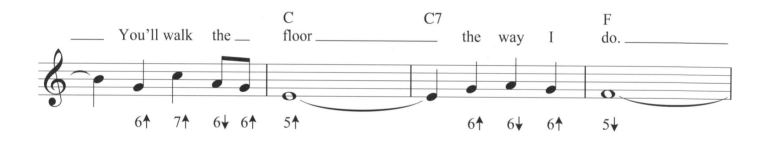

LET IT BE

Words and Music by JOHN LENNON
and PAUL McCARTNEY

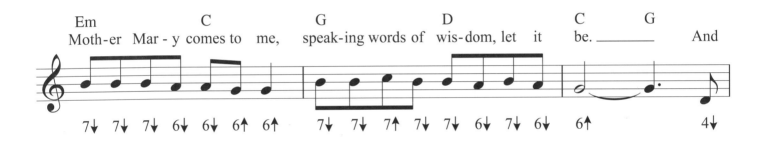

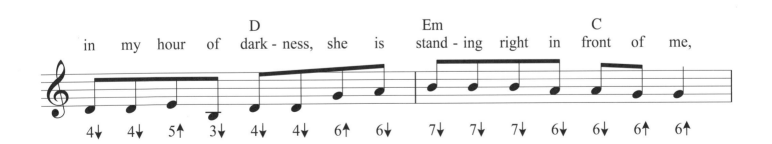

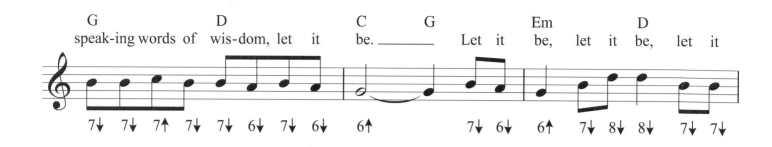

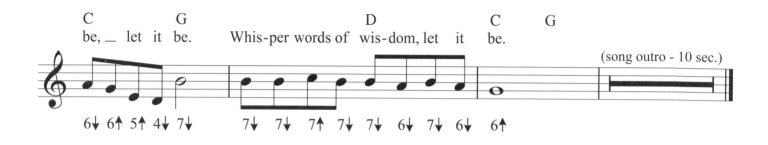

SUPERCALIFRAGILISTICEXPIALIDOCIOUS

from MARY POPPINS

Words and Music by RICHARD M. SHERMAN
and ROBERT B. SHERMAN

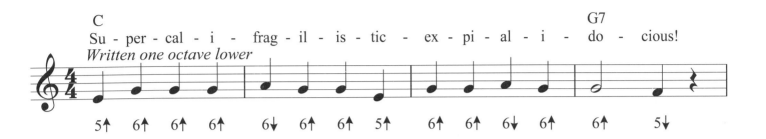

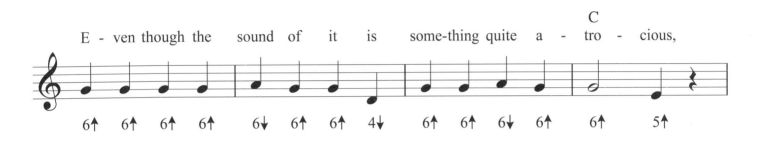

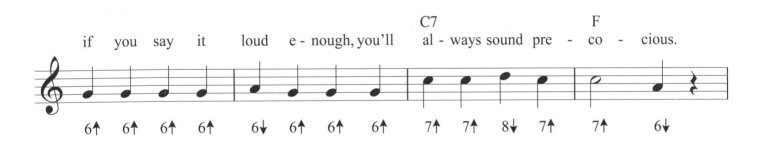

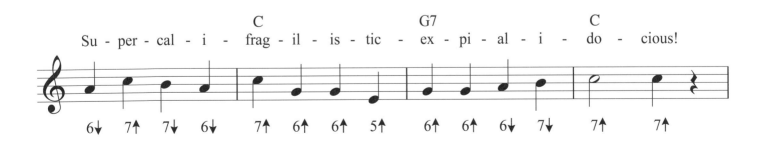

Um did - dle did - dle did - dle, um did - dle ay!

G7

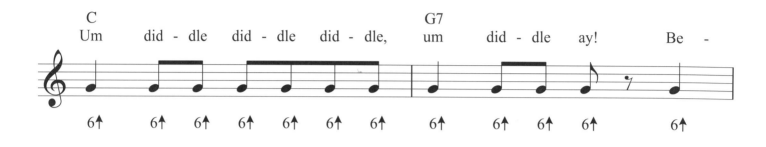

C
Um did - dle did - dle did - dle, um did - dle ay! Be -

G7

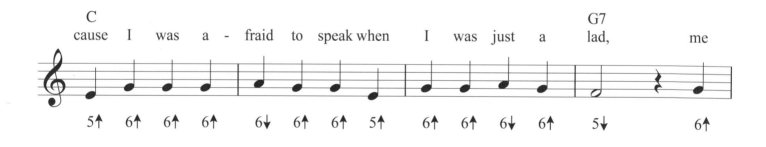

C
cause I was a - fraid to speak when I was just a lad, me

G7

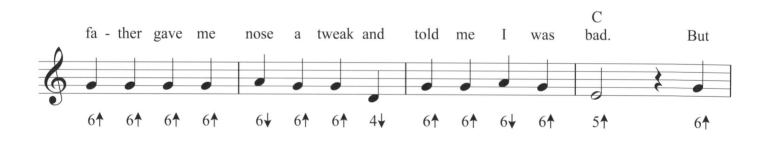

fa - ther gave me nose a tweak and told me I was bad. But

C

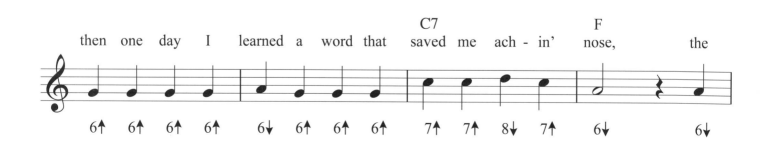

then one day I learned a word that saved me ach - in' nose, the

C7   F

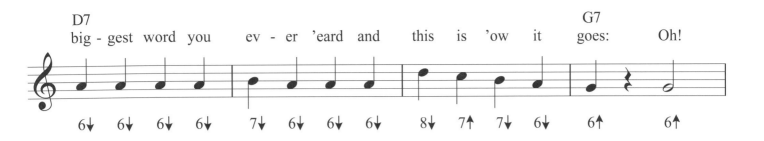

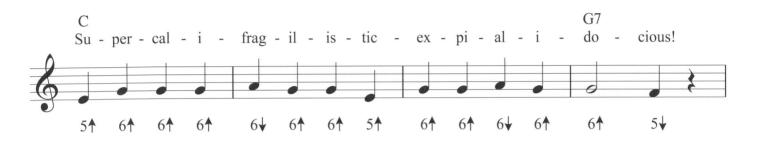

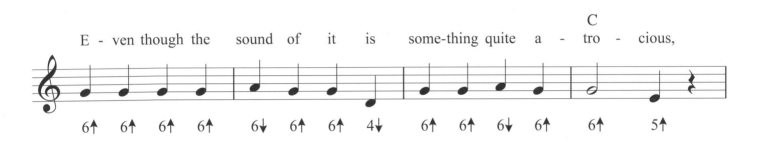

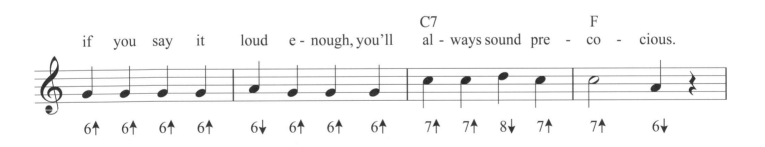

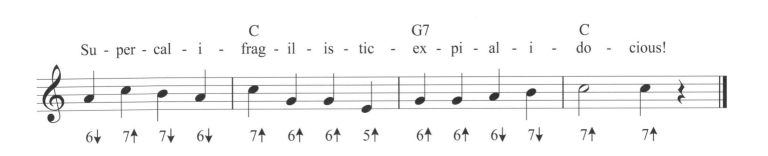

WE WILL ROCK YOU

Words and Music by BRIAN MAY

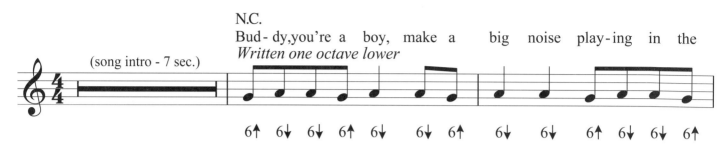

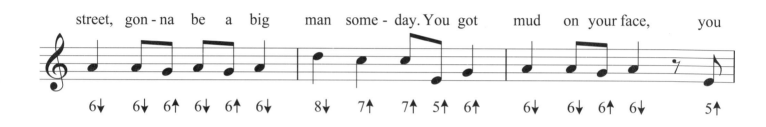

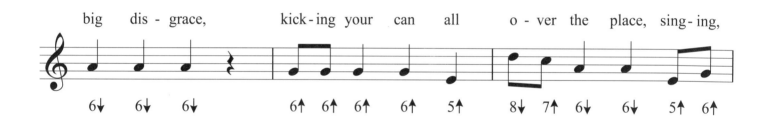

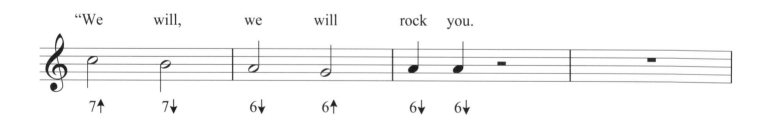

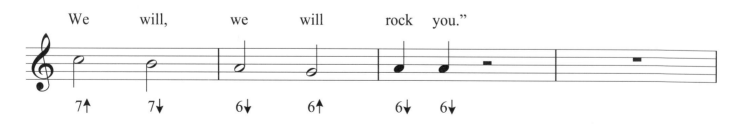

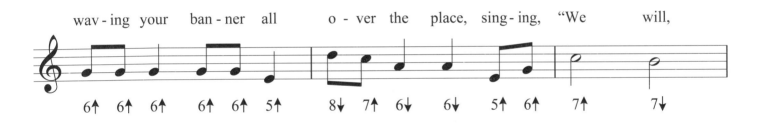

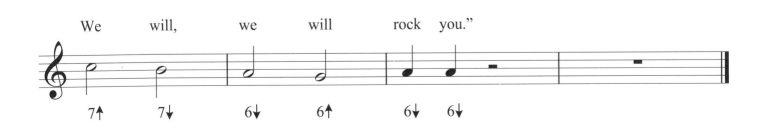

EVERY BREATH YOU TAKE

Music and Lyrics by STING

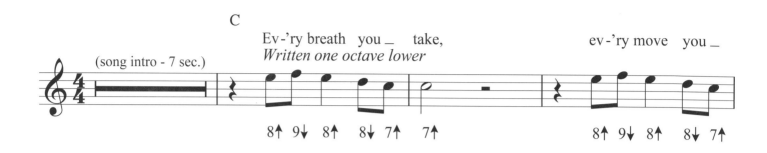

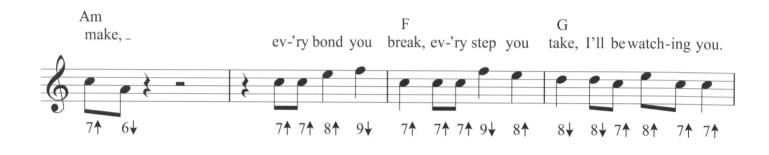

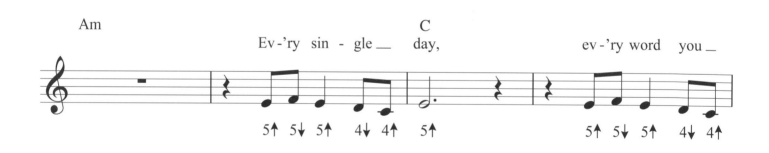

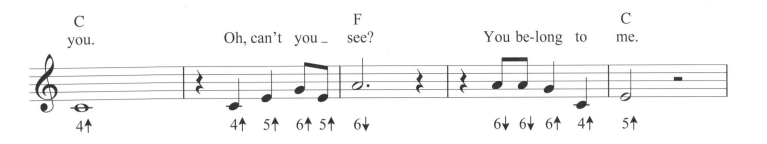

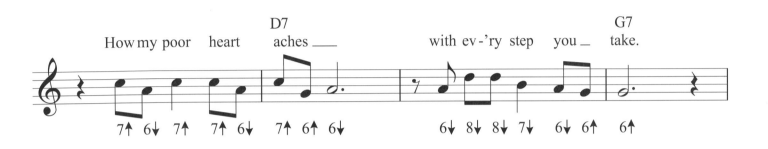

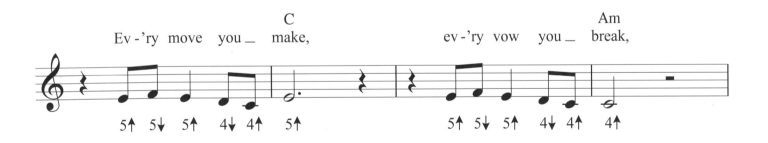

HAL LEONARD METHODS FOR KIDS

This popular series of method books for youngsters provides accessible courses that teach children to play their instrument of choice faster than ever before. The clean, simple page layouts ensure kids' attention remains on each new concept. Every new song presented builds on concepts they have learned in previous songs, so kids stay motivated and progress with confidence. These methods can be used in combination with a teacher or parent. The price of each book includes access to audio play-along and demonstration tracks online for download or streaming.

GUITAR FOR KIDS, METHOD BOOK 1
by Bob Morris and Jeff Schroedl

This method is equally suitable for students using electric or acoustic guitars. It features popular songs, including: Hokey Pokey • Hound Dog • I'm a Believer • Surfin' USA • This Land Is Your Land • Yellow Submarine • and more.
00865003 Book/Online Audio

GUITAR FOR KIDS, METHOD BOOK 2
by Chad Johnson

Equally suitable for children using electric or acoustic guitars, this book picks up where Book 1 left off. Songs include: Dust in the Wind • Eight Days a Week • Fields of Gold • Let It Go • Oye Como Va • Rock Around the Clock • and more.
00128437 Book/Online Audio

GUITAR FOR KIDS: BLUES METHOD BOOK
by Dave Rubin

Cool blues riffs, chords and solos are featured in this method, which is suitable for children using electric or acoustic guitars. Lessons include: selecting your guitar • parts of the guitar • holding the guitar • hand position • easy tablature • strumming & picking • blues riffs & chords • basic blues soloing • and more.
00248636 Book/Online Audio

GUITAR FOR KIDS SONGBOOK

This supplement follows chords in the order they are taught in book 1 of the guitar method. 10 songs: At the Hop • Don't Worry, Be Happy • Electric Avenue • Every Breath You Take • Feelin' Alright • Fly like an Eagle • Jambalaya (On the Bayou) • Love Me Do • Paperback Writer • Three Little Birds.
00697402 Book/Online Audio

GUITAR FOR KIDS METHOD & SONGBOOK
00697403 Book/Online Audio

BASS FOR KIDS METHOD BOOK
by Chad Johnson

Topics in this method book include selecting a bass, holding the bass, hand position, reading music notation and counting, and more. It also features popular songs including: Crazy Train • Every Breath You Take • A Hard Day's Night • Wild Thing • and more. Includes tab.
00696449 Book/Online Audio

DRUMS FOR KIDS METHOD BOOK

Topics included in this method book for young beginning drummers include setting up the drumset, music reading, learning rhthms, coordination, and more. Includes the songs: Another One Bites the Dust • Crazy Train • Free Fallin' • Living After Midnight • Old Time Rock & Roll • Stir It Up • and more.
00113420 Book/Online Audio

HARMONICA FOR KIDS METHOD BOOK
by Eric Plahna

Lessons include topics such as hand position, basic chord playing, learning melodies, and much more. Includes over 30 songs: All My Loving • Happy Birthday to You • Jingle Bells • Over the River and Through the Woods • Scarborough Fair • Take Me Out to the Ball Game • You Are My Sunshine • and more.
00131101 Book/Online Audio

PIANO FOR KIDS METHOD BOOK
by Jennifer Linn

This fun, easy course incorporates popular songs including: Beauty and the Beast • Heart and Soul • Let It Go • Over the Rainbow • We Will Rock You • and more classical/folk tunes. Topics covered include parts of the piano, good posture and hand position, note reading, dynamics and more.
00156774 Book/Online Audio

PIANO FOR KIDS SONGBOOK
by Jennifer Linn

A supplementary companion to the method book for piano, this book presents classic songs and contemporary hits which progress in like manner with the method book. Includes: All of Me • Can't Stop the Feeling • Do Re Mi • Linus and Lucy • and more.
00217215 Book/Online Audio

PIANO FOR KIDS CHRISTMAS SONGBOOK
by Jennifer Linn

Includes: Go, Tell It on the Mountain • I Want a Hippopotamus for Christmas • Jingle Bell Rock • Jingle Bells • Mary, Did You Know? • Rudolph the Red-Nosed Reindeer • Up on the Housetop • and more.
00238915 Book/Online Audio

UKULELE FOR KIDS
by Chad Johnson

This book features popular songs including: Barbara Ann • The Hokey Pokey • Rock Around the Clock • Yellow Submarine • You Are My Sunshine • and more. Lessons include: selecting your uke; parts of the uke; holding the uke; hand position; reading music notation and counting; notes on the strings; strumming and picking; and more!
00696468 Book/Online Audio

UKULELE FOR KIDS SONGBOOK

Strum your favorite hits from Jason Mraz, Disney, U2 and more! This collection can be used on its own, as a supplement to the *Ukulele for Kids* method book or any other beginning ukulele method. Songs: Don't Worry, Be Happy • I'm Yours • The Lion Sleeps Tonight • Riptide • The Siamese Cat Song • and more.
00153137 Book/Online Audio

UKULELE FOR KIDS METHOD & SONGBOOK
00244855 Book/Online Audio

HAL•LEONARD®
www.halleonard.com

Prices, contents, and availability subject to change without notice.